Let me introduce you to Dusty Dan.

He was an okay guy, loved his mom, ate all his oatmeal. Just an okay guy. Then one day, he decided to rob a bank. Nothing went well after that. It was just that one thing he did wrong---besides tying his dad's shoe laces together, sassing his mom, drowning the ---well, maybe there were a few things; but mainly he was an okay guy.

Now, he's sitting in jail. Dusty needs to be saved from his problem. We, too, need to be saved. The Apostle Paul in the Bible wrote about Dusty Dan (well, people like him; well, actually all of us). We all have disobeyed God and need Salvation.

Salvation is simple; but for us to understand all that the Eternal God has done for us, God turned the word 'salvation' into many words.

Let's let Dusty Dan show us some of the wonderful words that describe our Salvation.

Micah Understands Salvation

Beverly Ostrowski

This reference manual is dedicated to Micah, Olivia, J.W., Tyler, Nathan and Asher who inspired its concept, shaped its content, and argued its claims.

The drawings were by Micah. Biblical definitions were approved by Rev L. Duncan, M.Div. Graphic and technical support was provided by Greg Ostrowski.

I'd like to thank my editing service, bandbwriting@gmail.com, for polishing the manuscript and interfacing with the publisher.

Above all, this book was completed through the care and expertise of Betty Lou Duncan. Her commitment and insight of this project are seen throughout the book.

Copyright 2010 by the author

All rights reserved. No part of this publication may be reproduced or transmitted in any form or by any means without written permission of the author.

The room smelled of leather saddles, bees wax and a hint of nostalgia. Horseshoes hung amid the yellowed pictures dotting the walls. Some of the pictures were of a young man in an old-fashioned baseball uniform swinging his bat, hoping for a home run. Micah felt he had stepped back into history.

He still couldn't believe that he was standing in Dusty Dan's ranch office. He stood by the window watching the horses prance in the paddock attended by barking dogs. His grandfather's ranch; years before, Dusty Dan's ranch. Micah was visiting his grandfather for the first time. The majestic ranch was fun; horseback riding, swimming in the pond, fishing in the lake. Everything a boy could want. It was glorious.

As he turned back into the room, he studied the turn of the century room. His eyes fell on an old Navaho rug. It covered the scratches and stains on the hardwood floors answering to years of spurs and saddle bags. The stone fireplace across the room had warmed many a night. Mounted above the hand-carved mantle was an old baseball bat. The large crack down its side spoke of a long baseball past.

Micah was drawn to Dusty's photographs covering every wall of the ranch office as he waited for Grandfather to find the key to the ancient roll-top desk. The pictures that interested him most were of Dusty's glory days with the Boston Americans, back when baseball was played in corn fields and cow pastures. Micah, a left-handed slugger in his own right, had never visited his grandfather's ranch before; but he had heard a lot about Dusty Dan, his grandfather's grandfather. Something was missing, though. There were no pictures of a drifter in jail. It was as if it never happened.

"Is this really Dusty Dan?" Micah pointed to the faded newspaper account of the first World Series champions.

"The one in the middle, next to Cy Young," said Grandfather with pride as he rummaged through the desk. "Grandpa Dan was crazy for baseball."

"Is this the baseball he used?" Micah noticed an old frayed baseball on the trophy shelf. "It must be worth a fortune!"

"Probably is. But he had one thing more valuable. Here, let me show it to you."

Finally locating the large gold key, Grandfather opened the roll top desk in the corner. Inside was a worn, scruffy book. He reverently handed it to the boy. Micah studied the spider-webbed handwriting carefully. *My Story in Eleven Words,* by Dusty Dan. He turned the cracked brown-edged pages.

"Why did he use these big words, Grandfather?"

"He learned them from Apostle Paul in the Bible. These eleven special words brought him to this ranch. More importantly, they brought him into God's family. You see, baseball wasn't the most important thing in Dusty's life. It was belonging to a family. Now in God's family, he belongs and is greatly loved. Forever. Someday I'll introduce you to him.

"Here, let me explain these words to you and then I'll tell you the story of my grandfather, the legendary Dusty Dan."

Mercy
Showing pity for someone who doesn't deserve it.

Mercy
Showing pity for someone who doesn't deserve it.

God does: everything   **Me: nothing**

God looked down from Heaven. He saw that we had continuously disobeyed Him (sinned). Since there can be no sin in heaven, we wouldn't be able to live there with Him. Oops! It gets worse.

There is no way we can clean up our own sin. Only someone who has never sinned could remove it. He would have to take our punishment.

God felt sorry for us (**mercy**). He was concerned with the misery brought on by the sinner because of his sin.

Mercy is not getting the bad stuff we deserve.

Ephesians 2:4,5 *"But God, being rich in **mercy**, because of His great love with which He loved us . . . made us alive together with Christ."*

I Peter 1:3 *"Blessed be the God and Father of our Lord Jesus Christ, who according to His great **mercy** has caused us to be born again . . . through the resurrection of Jesus Christ from the dead."*

Grace
Joyfully doing something nice for someone who doesn't deserve it.

Grace

Joyfully doing something nice for someone who doesn't deserve it.

God does: everything   **Me: nothing**

God sent His only son, Jesus, to take the punishment for all our wrongs (sins). Since Jesus was all God and all Man, He was the only one that could do this.

Guess what! It's a free gift to us. It's the gift of living with God in Heaven forever.

Grace is getting the good stuff we don't deserve.

Romans 3:24a "(We are) *justified as a gift by His (God's)* **grace**.*"*

I Corinthians 1:4 Apostle Paul writes: *"I thank my God . . . for the* **grace** *of God which was given you in Christ Jesus."*

Ephesians 2:4b, 5b *"God . . . because of His great love with which He loved us . . . made us alive together with Christ, by* **grace** *you have been saved."*

Faith
Believing that everything God is and says is true.

Faith
Believing that everything God is and says is true.

God: waits patiently   **Me: trust in Him**

Isn't it great that all the amazing things God has planned for His children in the Bible can happen for us?

God has offered us this magnificent gift called salvation. Like all gifts, it's no good to us unless we take it. Shall we believe Him when He offers it to us?

Think about it, would God send His Son to our little planet to die a horrible death if it wasn't necessary? Would He put His plan in the Bible that took thousands of years to write, if it wasn't true? Just trust (**faith**) Him.

If we believe God and His Book (Bible) we have **faith**. It's true.

Hebrews 11:1 *"Now **faith** is the assurance of things hoped for, the conviction of things not seen."*

Ephesians 2:8 *"For by grace you have been saved through **faith**; and that not of yourselves, it is the gift of God."*

Repentance
A turning *from* sin and turning *to* God.

Repentance
A turning *from* sin and turning *to* God.

God: still waits   **Me: change sides**

So here we are. God wants us in His family. Jesus paid the penalty for our sins. We believe that He can make us clean.

If we're sorry for all the ways we disobeyed God (sorry means that we wished we hadn't done them and don't want to do them again), what are we waiting for?

Let's tell Him. You won't believe all the things that will happen *all at once*: justification, sanctification, redemption, righteousness, regeneration, reconciliation, etc. All together they're called Salvation!

Acts 26:20b *"that they should **repent** and turn to God."*
II Corinthians 7:10 *"For the sorrow . . . produces a **repentance** ... leading to salvation."*
Jesus said in Luke 24:46-47 *"Christ should suffer and rise again . . . and that **repentance** for forgiveness of sins should be proclaimed."*
Luke 15:7 *"there will be more joy in heaven over one sinner who **repents**, than over ninety-nine . . . who need no repentance."*

Justification
To declare or pronounce someone without guilt and right with God .

Justification
To declare or pronounce someone without guilt and right with God .

God does: everything **Me: nothing**

When God sees us now that we've repented, Jesus stands between us and God so all He sees is Jesus' perfection. Wow! All He sees in our life is a clean page. Like a judge in a court, He declares us innocent and pure because of Jesus. We are "right" in His sight.

Remember—only pure people can live in heaven. You don't really want robbers, cheaters and stinkers there, do you?

Romans 3:28 *"...a man is **justified** by faith apart from works of the Law."*

Romans 5:9 *"having now been **justified** by His blood, we shall be saved from the wrath of God through Him (Jesus)."*

Romans 5:1 *"having been **justified** by faith, we have peace with God through our Lord Jesus Christ."*

First I was born in my Parent's Family

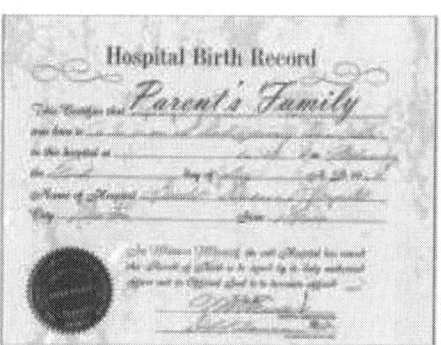

Now I also belong in God's Family

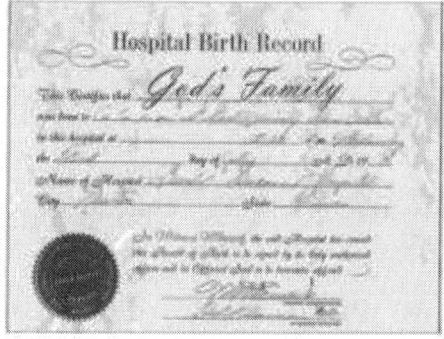

Born Again (Regeneration)
To be born a second time; this time in God's family.

Born Again (Regeneration)
To be born a second time; this time in God's family.

God does: all **Me: nothing**

Have you noticed that rich kids get to go awesome places and have awesome things just because their parents are wealthy? Well, now we are part of a wealthy family.

When we *repented* and asked to be part of God's family, we got all kinds of good things. They are all written in the Bible.

God has a map that shows the best road ahead. God can see what's going to happen to us tomorrow and the next day and the next. If we let Him, He will guide us around the potholes and give us life without worry. Honestly. Isn't that great!

Jesus said, John 3:3 *". . . unless one is **born again**, he cannot see the kingdom of God."*

I Peter 1:3 *"God . . . according to His great mercy has caused us to be **born again**."*

I Peter 1:23 *"for you have been **born again** . . . through the living and abiding word of God."*

Redemption
Payment to have something returned.

Redemption
Payment to have something returned.

God does: everything   **Me: nothing**

God created us to belong to Him. The first man (Adam) was without sin. Then he disobeyed God. Ever since, all of us are born wanting to disobey God.

The wrong things we have thought or done (sin) has tied us up. God bought us back (**redeemed us**) through His only son's death on the cross. How important to Him we are!

Rom: 3:23-24 *"for all have sinned and fall short of the glory of God, being justified as a gift by His grace through the* **redemption** *which is in Christ Jesus."*

Ephesians 1:7 *"In Him (Jesus) we have* **redemption**, . . . *the forgiveness of our trespasses (sins), according to the richness of His grace."*

Colossians 1:14 *"in whom (Jesus) we have* **redemption,** *the forgiveness of sins."*

Sanctification
To set apart to begin making clean and perfect.

Sanctification
To set apart to begin making clean and perfect.

God does: set us apart; start cleaning us up
   Me: examine my life for displeasing things

Since we've decided not to be stinkers anymore, we need to check out the way we think and the things we do. It isn't that hard. As we read the book God wrote for us, we can see what pleases Him. Since He promised never to leave us, He'll help us.

Have you noticed that people that are together a lot (like some grandparents) sometimes think alike; act alike? That's the way it is with **sanctification**. The more time we spend talking to God and reading His book, the more we'll be like Him.

Hebrews 12:14b *"the **sanctification** without which no one will see the Lord."*
I Thessalonians 4:7 *"God has not called us for the purpose of impurity, but in **sanctification**."*
Philippians 1:6 *"For I am confident of this very thing, that He who began a good work in you will perfect it until the day of Christ Jesus."*
Philippians 2:13 *"for it is God who is at work in you, both to will and to work for His good pleasure."*

Righteousness
Standards of a higher authority.
What is needed to make everything right with God.

Righteousness
Standards of a higher authority.
What is needed to make everything right with God.

God does: everything   **Me: nothing**

Okay, we've asked God to forgive our sins. We've asked to be part of His family. We want to please Him and not ourselves. So, how does that work?

God has standards like we have in our own family. God set up creation a certain way so it would work correctly.

He also set up salvation a certain way so we could live with a holy God eternally. He wrote the standards down in a book, the Bible. As a part of His family, we have His rightness (**righteousness**).

Romans 3:22a *". . . the **righteousness** (rightness) of God through faith in Jesus Christ for all those who believe."*

Romans 5:21 *"as sin reigned (was king) in death, even so grace might reign through **righteousness** to eternal life through Jesus Christ our Lord.*

II Corinthians 5:21 *"He (God) made Him (Jesus) who knew no sin to be sin on our behalf, that we might become the **righteousness** (rightness) of God in Him."*

Reconciliation
To bring God and man together in one family.

Reconciliation
To bring God and man together in one family.

God: opens His arms   **Me: run to God**

God said that when we're His child we never need to be anxious about anything.

He can take care of everything. He'll laugh with us in the good times and stay with us in all the hard times. In fact, He'll be with us all the time. God is eagerly waiting with open arms for us to hurry to Him and be **reconciled**.

Romans 5:10a, 11a *"For while we were enemies (away from God), we were **reconciled** to God through the death of His Son . . . And not only this, but we also exult (rejoice) in God through our Lord Jesus Christ, through whom we have now received the **reconciliation**."*

II Corinthians 5:17, 18a *"if any man is in Christ, he is a new creature; the old things passed away; behold, new things have come. Now all these things are from God, who **reconciled** us to Himself through Christ."*

II Thessalonians 3:3 *"But the Lord is faithful, and He will strengthen and protect you from the evil one."*

Glorification
God's brilliance, splendor and honor.

Glorification
God's brilliance, splendor and honor.

God is: everything   **Me: enjoying it with Him**

Are you getting tired of skinned knees, losing baseball games, cleaning the garage? Don't you wish you could just spend all your time with someone you enjoy?

God decided that all His children should be together. He's made each of us a special place in His house in heaven. No more scary, or sad or painful things will ever happen to us. Everything will always be perfect. All the time.

How exciting it will be to have new bodies that can do awesome things we've never even thought of -- forever. We'll live in God's own house with His splendor, brilliance, majesty. His **glory**.

Revelation 21:10-11, 23 *"the holy city, having the **glory** of God. Her brilliance was like a very costly stone, as a stone of crystal-clear jasper . . . no need of the sun or moon, for the **glory** of God has illumined (lit) it."*

Philippians 3:20a, 21 *"For our citizenship is in heaven from which also we eagerly wait for a Savior, the Lord Jesus Christ, who will transform the body of our humble state into conformity with the body of His **glory**.*

The Adventures of Dusty Dan

"Get yourself in that cell, Dusty Dan. Don't get too comfortable. Tomorrow you're gonna' hang!" The sheriff, with a final push, deposited Dusty in a dark, cold, gray concrete cell. Dusty Dan sat on his bed, his last day alive, and thought about all the things he'd done wrong. Robbin' that bank had been bad; almost killing the teller, the worst. What had put him on the wrong side of the law? Was he always bad? Somewhere deep inside, it seemed to Dusty that there had been good things in his life—he just couldn't remember where or when.

He thought of his dad, mean and sneaky. Dusty knew dark things about his dad that no one else knew. Did Dusty have all that dark inside him, too? Was he so bad he could never be good? Would he have to be just like his father? Well, he would never know. Tomorrow he would hang and be dead and gone. But gone where?

A dog barked. An owl hooted. It was dark outside. It was dark in the cell. Dusty was all alone. Cold and alone.

Meanwhile across town, Judge Landry wasn't sleeping so well himself. As he had told his wife at dinner, "I hate to see a man hanged and I especially hate to be the one to do it. This guy, just a kid really, seems real nice. It's a shame, a real shame."

"Just think, dear," she replied. "if you don't, the man will rob and steal again. Then more people will suffer. You must pass judgment on that man. Can you do that?"

"Sure Martha," he sighed, "being a judge, I must decide if he's guilty or innocent. Guilty, he's hanged no matter what a nice guy he is. All sin must be punished. Yep, I've seen the evidence. He's guilty. Still, it's a shame."

##

Morning came too soon for Judge Landry and even more so for Dusty Dan. He couldn't eat the oatmeal the deputy slid through the bars. It tasted cold and sticky, like yesterday's wet newspaper. Too soon the jingle of the jail keys and the scraping of old spurs announced the sheriff. A large rusty key slid into the cell's iron lock, tearing at Dusty's heart. Finally, the door creaked wide open, sealing his fate.

"Dusty, get up!"

"Yea, yea."

"You're free to go."

"What? I'm what?"

"Said you're free to go. The judge declared you **justified**. That means he can't find the evidence against you. It's as if you never did anything wrong."

"But I'm, I'm…"

"Get out of here before I charge you with clutterin' up my jail."

Dusty grabbed his shoes and ran out. The sun hit him in the eyes. He breathed in the fresh air. It was wonderful. He pulled his baseball out of his pocket and tossed it in the air. He danced along the road leading to the makeshift sandlot.

Free! Free!

Until—

waiting under a tree was his friend, Pete.

##

"Hey, Dusty, the sheriff said you were set free. Come on, I've found a good bank to rob in the next town."

Dusty shook his head, lowering his eyes.

"Nope, I'm sorry I ever robbed the first one. Very sorry. I want to change. From now on, I'm going to do what's right."

"What *is* right?"

"I don't know but I'm gonna look for it until I find it. I think it has to do with obeying rules; man's rules and God's rules." Dusty turned away and skipped down the opposite road. He had experienced **repentance** and it felt good. Really good.

He hadn't gone too far when he felt a gun in his back. A gruff voice whispered in his ear to be quiet. Rough ropes bound his hands while a dirty kerchief was stuffed in his mouth. He didn't have time to wonder what was happening. A blow to the head took him into oblivion.

"Look what I got, Mom. The guy that shot me in the arm in the robbery. Now we can do him over good."

Dusty opened one eye and looked cautiously around him. He was on the rough plank floor of a small cabin. It smelled strangely of cleaning soap and beef stew.

"No, son, if the judge pronounced him innocent, he can't be punished for the crime anymore. It's like the judge couldn't see all the bad Dusty had done. We have to let him go. First, let's see if we can help him. Jake, find your old clothes and give 'um to this young man."

"What! After what he did? That's not fair."

"Jake, it's called **Grace**, doin' somethin' good for somebody that he don't deserve."

"Well, what's it called not beating him up? Or feelin' sorry for somebody who doesn't deserve it?"

"**Mercy,** Jake, it's called mercy."

Jake didn't have his mother's mercy or grace. He followed Dusty out of the cabin with his bag of clothes and a basket of ham and cornpone. He tried to think of a plan. He had heard of a place in the big city where rich people would buy criminals and make them slaves. Might as well get some money out of this, he thought. But as he started down the trail following Dusty, he heard his mother calling him.

"You get back in this cabin, Jake. I need some wood chopped." So Jake let Dusty shuffle down the road alone. He'd find him another day.

Dusty walked for days. His feet burned on the dry hot road. His throat was parched. Finally, tired and hungry, he went to sleep under a large tree. Its branches draped down over him like a curtain. Like his mother's worn window curtain; shading him from the night rain, and later, the morning sun. He was still there when he heard a strong, pleasant voice say, "Well, what have we got here? Where are you headed to, young man?"

"Nowhere. Just wandering around. Looking for a home."

"Then come with me. My ranch can be your home. That is, if you decide to follow the standards of my ranch. They are easy rules, but they must be followed. They make everything right at my ranch. Oh, by the way, I'm Mr. Jennings. Come along now. We'll get you home."

"Oh, yes, sir. Yes, sir. I'll do all the **rightness** of the ranch."

Everything went fine at Mr. Jennings' ranch. That is until dinner time. Dusty's hair was wet and slicked back, his clothes torn but fairly clean and he smelled of lye soap as he sat down to the table. He didn't know how to use a napkin or even a fork. He wanted to do right but didn't know how. Everyone at the table laughed at him trying to lift food into his mouth on a fork.

Mr. Jennings understood Dusty's problem. "Dusty," he said. "I'm going to set you apart from everyone else so we can get you cleaned up. It's called **sanctification**----setting apart to clean up."

Early the next morning, Dusty went to Miss Prissly's house nearby to learn grooming and table manners. He was determined not to embarrass Mr. Jennings again. For almost two weeks, Dusty went to Miss Prissly's until one morning---.

Just as he closed the gate from Mr. Jennings' ranch, Dusty again felt a gun in his back. He groaned as his hands were tied and he was lifted onto a horse. Jake had found him.

##

The sun was high two days later when Dusty stood on a platform, the heat scorching his head, sweat dripping from his bare chest. Waiting to be sold as a slave. Maybe the judge hadn't punished him, but he wasn't so sure about Jake. The air smelled of sweaty flesh, vomit, and things Dusty was glad he wasn't sure of. He closed his eyes, trying to ignore the loud bidding of the slave owners around him. After a time, big burly hands took him off the platform and untied him. A strong, pleasant voice, Mr. Jennings' voice, spoke.

"I just bought you, Dusty. You belong to me again. Come along. We'll get you home."

"You bought me?"

"Well, you were mine, a part of my ranch. Then I lost you, and now I've found you. I had to pay to get you back---so I guess I **redeemed** you. I'm going to take you home to live with me. I'm glad we're back together. **Reconciliation** with you is important to me. Only this time, no one is going to take you away. I want you to be part of my family, Dusty. Is that all right with you?"

"I don't rightly know, Mr. Jennings. What does that mean? What will change?"

Mr. Jennings scratched his head a little.

"Well, let's see now. First things, you don't call me Mr. Jennings anymore. You call me Father, or better yet, Dad. You can always believe the things I teach you and can trust me to know what's best for you. That's **faith**. Then when I die, everything—the ranch, the house, the horses—everything will belong to you. Would you like that?"

"Wow! That's terrific. When can we do that?"

Mr. Jennings' eyes sparkled. He was so excited to have a son. "We can stop off at the judge's house on the way home."

"Ah, ah, there's something I have to tell you before we go there. I robbed a bank once and got caught. And was almost hanged."

"How can that be, Dusty? I went through all the records at the courthouse and there is no record of you committing a crime."

"The judge said, when he got ready to convict me, he couldn't find any evidence. So he made a court announcement that I was **justified.** That means there's no record of me ever doing wrong. I don't understand how that works."

"Actually, I knew about that, Dusty. There is no record because I paid the penalty for you. The judge told me of a young man, you, that needed someone to pay the price for his wrongs. His sins. I said I'd pay your debt. It's gone. We'll never have to worry about that again. See, the penalty was paid and you are forgiven. Once your sin is canceled, you can't be punished for it again. Now, let's go to the judge and get that paperwork started."

As the sun was setting, Mr. Jennings and Dusty Dan, father and son, rode toward the ranch. Dusty Dan Jennings sat tall in the saddle. He was a new person. He had a new name, a new life and a new home forever on a giant ranch. It was like being **born again**.

Dusty could see the ranch as he came to the top of the last hill. The sun made the windows of the ranch house sparkle like diamonds. Then, it danced over the porch, to the roof and beyond, sprinkling shimmer everywhere. The horses in the paddocks were rich in brown color; the grass beyond, a gleaming shamrock. Here was **glory**---a majestic ranch. He couldn't resist a wide smile.

Dusty Dan had finally come home.

##

Grandfather wiped the moisture from his eyes as he finished the story. He was staring out the window at the lush meadows and the rich paddocks. He was thinking of the change in Dusty, from jailbird to baseball hero.

"And now, Micah," he said as he rose from the rocker and stretched, "I have something special for you." Grandfather walked over to the trophy shelf and picked up the old, ragged baseball.

"Just before he died, my grandfather wrote on this ball and handed it to me. He said, 'Child, this is all you will ever need in life. Even beyond this life.'"

Grandfather handed the ball to Micah.

"What are the words written on it? Did a team sign it? Is it the winning baseball?"

Grandfather laughed. "Well, it is the winning ball, but not in the way you think. This ball helps me remember how my grandfather came to the ranch, and how I can get to his heavenly ranch.

"Oh, I now see. These are the words from Dusty's story. Wow, I wish I could have known him."

"Well, like I said before, I want you to meet him someday."

"I thought you said he died."

"He did, many years ago. My grandmother said he died with a smile on his face. He knew he was going to God's ranch in heaven. Everyone who has salvation will be there. I'll introduce you to him when you and I arrive. You understand the words on the baseball now?"

"I think so. But I still think Grandpa Dan used a lot of big words."

"Well, he didn't say them as much as he lived them. And that's what counts."

God's Plan of Salvation

Becoming a Christian is very easy.

**Simply, if you are sorry for your sins and want to be part of His family, just tell Him so, and He will take care of the rest.

Ask Him to forgive your sins, and then commit to follow God's guidance.**

When God made the first man (Adam), He gave him a spirit like God's spirit. When the Adam disobeyed Him, he lost his spiritlife with God. Getting this spiritlife back is called salvation.

Since God cannot allow sin, all wrongdoing must punished. Now we don't deserve to have someone to take the punishment for our sins, but God had **mercy** on us.

Jesus chose to take our punishment (**grace**) but we must agree to let Him (**faith**). Turning away from wrongdoing and turning to God is called **repentance.** Our disobedience is forgiven. God looks at us like we've never done anything wrong **(justification).** We have been reborn **(born again)**, into God's family. He buys us back from sin **(redemption)**, paying for our sins through Jesus' death on the cross. We are set apart from our past **(sanctification)** while God teaches us how to live right **(righteousness).** When we come back to God and have our spiritlife again, we have **reconciled** with Him. Some day we will be in our new home in heaven **(glory).** All of the promises God gives to those who obey Him are ours! There are so many – underline them as you read through your Bible and you will be amazed.

Salvation In Eleven Words

Mercy – undeserved forgiveness
Grace – undeserved gift
Faith – trust in God
Repentance – turn away from sin; turn to God
Justification – declare not guilty
Born Again – reborn spiritually
Redemption – to buy back
Sanctification – to set apart to cleanse
Righteousness–God's standards; His rightness
Reconciliation – to bring back together
Glorification – God's majesty

Can you match these words to the following stories?

1. Alice was very angry, she threw her mother's favorite heirloom vase across the room. When her Mother came home and opened the door, she gasp! The only remembrance she had of Grandmother lay in zillions of pieces. She looked up at Alice through her tears. "Did you do that on

purpose? Alice nodded, "I'm really sorry. I was so angry." Mother swept the pieces up, quietly repeating, "I'm so sorry you're hurting, Alice. I'm so sorry." Mother showed _____ to Alice.

2. Janice made a sculpture for the school auction. She drew sketches, bought clay and stayed up nights working on it. She hated to part with it, but she knew it was made for the auction. The next day, Janice secretly brought her savings to school to bid on the sculpture. It took all her savings, but she won the auction and took home the sculpture. She had _____ it.

3. Did you ever steal something and later wished you hadn't? Stella stole a paper weight with stars on it from her teacher's desk. Mrs. Reynolds was very disappointed in her when she found out. Stella wished she had never stolen the paper weight, and decided she would rather be honest than to steal. Stella _____ of her stealing.

4. Josh was on his way to the ice cream store. He could almost taste their chocolate almond ice cream cone. Danny suddenly stepped in front of him, causing him to fall and skin his knee. Danny laughed. Josh got up and continued on to the ice cream store. There he bought two ice cream cones. One for him and one for Danny; even though he didn't deserve it.

    Josh showed _____ to Danny.

5. Jamie didn't like Mike at all. Mike had been Jamie's best friend until the day he stole Jamie's four-color pen and said it was his own. Later, Jamie's mother sorted out his school papers and readied his school books to give away. Clipped to some old spelling pages was a pen—a four-color pen. Jamie hurried over to Mike's house with the pen to ask forgiveness. There, in the cluttered driveway, under the basketball hoop, they _____. Mike had been waiting for Jamie to find the truth. He had long ago forgiven him.

6. Do you ever feel like you've messed up your life so much that you'd like to go back to the hospital nursery and start all over again. I mean, begin your whole life over without some of the things you've done? That you could be _____?

7. The students jumped off desks, threw paper wads, punched each other. It was impossible to teach the class so she set standards. She imparted _____.

8. Mother took little Janie aside to scrub her clean. She had chocolate-covered cheeks, and was ready to wipe her hands on her starched dress. Janie was to be a flower girl in her sister's wedding. Mother beamed with satisfaction as Janie walked down the aisle scrubbed clean. Janie had been _____.

9. Bessie entered the museum reverently. She walked past all the important displays until she

reached the Queen's jewels. There they were in all their brilliance, sparkling from the window's sunlight. What majesty, what splendor, what honor they held. Wouldn't it be grand to be the Queen? Queens have such majesty, such _____.

10. Mother had to leave for work early, so she gave Judy the rent money to take to the landlord. Judy studied the big bills in the envelope. It was more money than she had ever seen. It could buy tons of ice cream or candy bars. Judy closed the envelope and licked it shut. She could never spend the money, her mother trusted her with it. Her mother had _____ in her.

11. Little Johnny was playing with matches and set the orphanage on fire. The headmaster knew who did it; but when he confronted him, a large tenth grader stepped between the headmaster and Johnny and took the blame. As the older boy was stripped and beaten, Johnny was free to leave. He was _____.

Word Search List

Word List:

Born again
Faith
Glorify
God
Grace
Justification
Love
Mercy
Reconciliation
Redemption
Repentance
Righteousness
Sanctification

Words About Salvation

```
j U s t i f i c a t i o n
v E a c s d q c z e r g o
x W n i a g a n r o b f i
a E c n a t n e p e r r t
c S t x z f t b n d c i a
h E i b q y f i r o l g i
m R f v x h u m s t r h l
v E i c n x q z u a n t i
d A c w h e m a c b n e c
q F a i t h e g r m s o n
t Z t b e c r w h j d u o
j D i k l z c q b d g s c
t L o v e w y x n q o n e
f X n n o i t p m e d e r
w I o w s c h a d x z s c
t C q s v b w m j a q s z
```

Word list on page 50

Crossword Clues:

Across:

3. God's standards; His rightness

6. Why God gave His Son for our salvation (John 3:16)

8. Undeserved gift

9. Trust in God

10. To turn away from sin and turn to God

11. Declare not guilty

Down:

1. Reborn spiritually

2. To bring back together

3. To buy back

4. God's majesty

5. To set apart to cleanse

7. Undeserved forgiveness

Words About Salvation

Clues on page 52

Clues on Page 52

Other books in **Kid's Theology** series:

Olivia Understands the Promise
Nathan Understands the Tabernacle
Asher Understands the Covenant
Anne Understands the Father
Lauren Understands Life as a Roman

Stony Creek Explorers series:
by B. L. Duncan

My Dad is Laid Off
I Feel Like a Wet Dog
The Puzzle Box
The Gluten Game
The Hideout
Monkey Bars and Magnets

Notes To Parents

This book is meant to help children understand more of God's Word. Sometimes in the Bible, these words are interchangeable in describing salvation in general. That does not take away from the richness that each word brings to the doctrine of salvation.

This resource can be used for devotions, character training, church camp, Sunday School, homeschooling, Christian schools, etc. Bible Verses are from the *New American Standard Bible*.

Answer key for stories:
1. mercy
2. redeemed
3. repented
4. grace
5. reconciled
6. born again (regeneration)
7. righteousness
8. sanctified
9. glory
10. faith
11. justified

Words About Salvation

Word search puzzle answer key:

```
j U s t i f i c a t i o n
  a                     o
  n i a g a n r o b     i
E c n a t n e p e r r   t
  t                 i   a
  i     y f i r o l g   i
  f             r h     l
  i           a   t     i
  c       m c     e     c
f a i t h e           o n
  t       r           u o
  i       c         g s c
l o v e   y         o n e
  n n o i t p m e d e   r
                        s
                        s
```

Words About Salvation

Crossword puzzle answer key:

				¹b			²r					
³r	i	⁴g	h	t	e	o	u	s	n	e	s	⁵s
e		l		r			c					a
d	⁶l	o	v	e		n		m		o		n
e		r		⁸g	r	a	c	e		n		c
m		i		o		⁷g		c		c		t
p		f		d		a		c		i		i
t		i		i		y		l				f
i		c		n				i				i
o	⁹f	a	i	t	h					a		c
n		t		¹⁰r	e	p	e	n	t			a
		i							t			t
		o							i			i
		n							o			o
¹¹j	u	s	t	i	f	i	c	a	t	i	o	n

Look for:

Asher Understands The Covenant

by Beverly Ostrowski

Look for:

Nathan Understands The Tabernacle

by Beverly Ostrowski

Look for:

Understands The Promise

By B. L. Duncan and Beverly Ostrowski

Look for:

Look for:

Stony Creek Explorers

I Feel Like a Wet Dog

by B.L. Duncan

Made in the USA
Charleston, SC
05 November 2016